SMART MARKETING

99 Small Steps to
Connect with Customers,
Grow Sales, and
Rise Above the Competition

Andrea Kamenca, MBA

Published by MindView Press:
ISBN 13: 978-0-9996807-0-4   eBook
ISBN-10:

ISBN 13: 978-0-9990214-0-9   paperback
ISBN-10: 0998021407

To my advisors, mentors, clients, and staff who taught me, challenged me, and supported me. Thank you.

Author's Note

I started a small business in May of 2008 literally six months prior to the BIG crash in September. I had always dreamed of owning a business and so embarked upon the encounter. I am humbled to say that I built the business from scratch to one with revenue ranked in the top 7% nation-wide. The reason I was able to do so was because I knew that even in a recession, every business needs more customers! And yet, marketing and sales do not come naturally to most business owners. The company I began was a marketing company.

I started with one client and when I sold the company, I had 155, including contracts with large and small businesses, and city and state governments. While I was building my lifelong dream, I learned a great deal about both strategic and tactical marketing and sales. I applied the lessons and steps to my business and my clients. It was a tough but rewarding time.

There is no other way to truly test your business skills and personal mettle than as a business owner, especially during the most difficult economic time in the last eighty years. As I pivoted and adjusted to the changing economy, it occurred to me that perhaps other business owners might be interested in my lessons learned. So, I wrote a blog about my experiences. Some of the lessons and steps shared in this book were shared on my blog when I owned Mind the Gap Marketing Solutions. Since then, I have owned three additional businesses. I have learned new steps that can help you grow your business.

It doesn't have to be difficult. Just take a few steps and watch your business grow!

P.S. Thank you for purchasing this book. If you would like occasional specials and announcements, please go to my website, www.andreakamenca.com. Also, if you liked the book, please leave an honest review on Amazon. It helps others readers and me know what worked and what didn't. Thanks!

Branding, Your business and You...Hint: It all starts with YOU!

The direction of your business, your ideal clients, your messaging, and your graphic design all begin with you. You must decide these critical aspects of your business or they will be determined by default. The small decisions made every day by each employee, vendor, client or prospective client add up to an overall feeling and impression. If you don't guide the process, THAT becomes your brand.

Once you have decided to steer the branding process, what do you do? To begin, make a list of the traits of your ideal client or clients. Include things like their market sectors, size, location, culture, and the way you interact with them.

Then, determine the messaging that resonates with them. What message, what value proposition makes them want to buy from you?

Next, review your graphics. Is the graphic design that represents your firm consistent? Does it appeal to you? Does it reflect your firm? Is it appealing to your ideal client?

Finally, how is your client treated? Every person, every point of contact between your business and your client is a moment of clarity and decision for your prospective client.

Decisiveness and consistency are more important than extreme creativity and breaking new ground. Ideally, all aspects will be incorporated but the decision is yours.

1. **Describe your 'brand.'**
2. **Create a profile of your ideal customer**
3. **Identify your value proposition (what makes your business special or different from the competition)**
4. **Develop messaging that persuasively describes your value proposition to your ideal customer**
5. **Incorporate messaging into your brand.**

Business Planning, Culture, and Leadership to Drive Results

Mastering Rockefeller Habits, a book by Vern Harnish, was one of the best books I have ever read about creating a business structure around action, core values, people, goals, and results.

Working to live core values in a small business can be particularly challenging when the pressures of cash flow, payroll, and limited time sometimes try to trump higher values. Yet, business core values are so important that in my view, why have your own business if you cannot live the values that you espouse. Every business reflects the values of its leadership.

When I was working for IBM, Lou Gerstner was the CEO. He was phenomenal. He stood for entrepreneurship, action, results, and shareholder value. He is largely credited with saving IBM. About six months to a year before I left IBM, Mr. Gerstner left IBM. I saw in as little as two months, cultural changes starting to occur under new leadership. Bureaucracy started seeping back into the organization. Decision making slowed. Given that IBM boasts 370,000 employees and probably at least 12-17 levels between the top and bottom of the company, the cultural change was lightning fast. It stands to reason that companies with as little as 2-10 employees will feel the core values of the leadership even more powerfully.

Mind the Gap employed the one-page business plan and the quarterly themes, core values, BHAG, and metrics in order to grow the company and applied its core values to business on a daily basis.

6. **Use a One-page business plan**

7. **Decide your core values**

8. **Set out your Big, Hairy, Audacious Goals**

9. **Describe the measures or metrics you will use to measure your success.**

Marketing Strategy, Marketing Goals, Marketing Tactics: Fundamental to Business Success

Clearly defined mission, goals, strategies and tactics are the foundation of a business. The marketing decisions should flow from those fundamentals. Whether you implement a new marketing collateral piece or search engine optimization, asking the question, "Does it get us where we want to go?" will prevent you from chasing the latest, greatest technology or tool for its own sake. Ultimately, marketing tactics should have a return on investment associated with them.

Many business people are familiar with the terminology listed above. However, their application to individual businesses is often unclear. It is as critical to understand and define these terms for your business as it is to understand the state of your accounts receivable. A business's mission, goals, strategy and tactics create its foundation and give it the footings to support a large and evolving business structure.

"Mission," a term used heavily in the 1990's, usually consisted of a very long sentence developed by a committee in a boardroom or on a retreat. The drafters of these missions sought to bring clarity and purpose to their companies. Too often, however, the missions consisted of confusing statements with competing components that, in turn, resulted in some serious 'eyeball rolling' by staff. The simplest mission statements are the most helpful. For example, "Greenstreet Construction builds quality retail structures." Missions are stated as though they are already occurring, even if they are not. A mission's purpose is to state why you are in business and, frequently, includes your firm's values.

Goals are defined as measurable milestones that drive the performance of the business. A goal is, "sign contracts with three retail developers for projects in excess of $5 million in the next six months." A goal has specific numbers tied to it. Revenue, profitability, time, and other quantitative assessments can and should be components of goals.

After you and your colleagues craft and commit to the firm's mission and goals, develop strategy to implement the mission and achieve the goals. A clearly defined strategy answers the "how?" to achieving your firm's mission and goals. Strategy, simply put, is the direction in which your company is headed, while considering your services, your competitors' services, opportunities in the marketplace, your strengths and weaknesses, and those of your competitors. Strategy defines the markets you are trying to penetrate and how you are positioning your company against the competition.

Ordinarily, you should strive to fill a market niche. Greenstreet Construction, for example, could state its strategy in the following way: To establish itself as experts in constructing retail establishments that are categorized as "big box," strip centers, and mixed-use.

Yet, even the most compelling mission, goals and strategy mean nothing without action. Tactics, represent that action. Tactics execute the firm's strategy. Tactics typically involve more practical marketing decisions, like which type of advertising to purchase, where to spend your marketing dollars, and what type of prospects to target. Most firms, especially small ones, spend most of their time on tactics.

In fact, when businesses get in trouble, they concentrate their focus on tactics. It can be tempting for principals and marketing professionals to feel as though they are making progress when they are actively placing advertising, creating direct mail campaigns, preparing proposals and "doing lunch."

Greenstreet Construction's tactics will include placing at least six advertisements in publications widely read by retail developers; creating relationships with the top 10 retail developers; meeting with at least six architecture firms that design retail; and developing and executing a marketing campaign informing their prospective clients about their successes in the marketplace.

Once you determine your mission, goals and strategy and apply the appropriate tactics, your results will multiply and exponential growth will soon follow. The firm will have a focus, as will the people within it. The mission, goals, and strategy will establish an atmosphere where specific, measurable success can occur.

10. Write a mission statement.

11. Develop three goals that include specifics like revenue, costs, and timelines.

12. Answer the question 'how will you achieve these goals?'

Marketing Strategy: The Importance of a Niche

Whether it's architecture, construction, music or law, the survivors in this economy are ones that have a well-defined niche.

During the last boom, most companies resisted creating a niche for themselves. They wanted to be as many things to as many people as possible. And, the market wasn't particularly punitive if they weren't well-niched. Well, it is now.

The companies surviving and even thriving in this economy are ones that chose their niche based on their expertise, the market demand, and the competitive landscape. One of my valued clients, SportsPLAN Studio, is thriving in this economy because they are specialists in sports architecture. With over 500 projects to their name, they are truly specialists. This economy has affected them but they are surviving, even thriving, in this market.

There are other companies that folded under the stress of the great recession. The reason? They had a niche but it was one too closely tied to market demand that was speculative. Consider the robustness and the longevity of the market as part of choosing your niche.

There are others who have chosen a niche that is saturated but with style and purpose they have risen above. For example, in the music industry, The Arizona Republic quoted Chris Sampson, dean of the popular music program at the University of Southern California (my grad school alma mater) as saying about Beyoncé', Taylor Swift, and Lady Gaga, "What has made each successful is that they have carved out a very specific niche for themselves. That comes from that level of focus, knowing who they are artistically, and almost as a brand."

Others choose niches that are tiny in terms of competitors but big enough to support the business and the mission of the owners. For example, PK Bootmaker, a specialized boot maker in Southern Arizona has a unique and somewhat "tiny" niche but has been successful in dominating the custom boot market.

When I emphasized this point to clients they resisted. Heck, even I resisted with my firm. Yet, it is critical to choose your business niche and dominate it. The chances of surviving, thriving, and then, dominating your market are much higher and long-term success is more likely.

13. Identify your niche.

Multi-Pronged Marketing...Why Just One or Two Marketing Tactics Are Not Enough

Many clients when they first came to our office wanted a website or a brochure or a logo. The first thing we asked them was to articulate their goal for the website, brochure, or logo. They usually said that they wanted more business or were going to a trade show or perhaps they had a potential client they want to impress. And, that is where the strategic marketing discussion begins.

The reality is that just one unfocused marketing tactic or activity rarely achieves the desired results. The mistake a lot of businesses make is to implement a reactionary marketing plan or, in some cases, what we call "Hail Mary Marketing." In other words, you have implemented little or no marketing tactics and all of a sudden you need to implement something so you pick something easy...an ad in the yellow pages, a coupon in one of those mailers to people's homes. I once had an upscale lawyer from a higher end firm in California consider putting fliers on people's car windshields! This wasn't a personal injury practice...they practiced water and environmental law!

Marketing that makes an impact must be implemented with a thoughtful strategy behind it. The market sector, the action you want to provoke, the type of clients you want to attract, these are all important questions to ask and answer before you spend money on marketing. After you answer these questions, it is critical that you choose more than one tactic to implement. In other words, a direct mailer with email marketing and a press release will work together to make a bigger market impression. You are more likely to reach more people. You are also likely to reach people more often. In graduate school, they teach that advertising should be evaluated through the constructs of Reach and Frequency. Marketing is no different.

When I was selling to doctors, I ensured they heard my message at least four times from four different sources in a six week time period. They sometimes quoted my materials back to me! Because when people hear the marketing message from different sources, it feels like there are many people providing the same message. It feels less like marketing and more like education or awareness.

In short, if you want to make an impact with your marketing: 1) Create a strategy and goals. 2) Implement multiple tactics.

14. Articulate your strategy.

15. List the tactics you will use to support your marketing strategy.

Market Sharper. Market Smarter. Market Harder.

Today's economy demands both a return to basics, as well as a call to update, reenergize and refresh. It is NOT the time to reduce marketing expenses and lay off sales staff. Instead it is time to evaluate everything within the context of your return on investment (ROI.) In this economy, there are three things to do, market sharper, market smarter, and market harder.

Market Sharper.

Make this the year that you create and implement marketing and sales plans. Hold yourself and your people accountable to goals that are both qualitative and, very importantly, quantitative. Revisit past sales and marketing strategies and assess their effectiveness. With those results in mind, plan for the future keeping in mind the economy.

Market Smarter.

Investigate and try techniques, tools, and areas you have not explored or investigated including new markets, new marketing approaches, or new technology. Increase your knowledge about website functionality, search engine optimization, social networking, and the latest in proposal, advertising or sales trends. Look at the demographics.

Understand your markets and how they buy and communicate.

Market Harder.

Make every day and every moment count. Make extra calls. Submit more proposals. Put out more materials. Look for every opportunity to gain exposure and attention for your firm. Stay in front of clients as much as possible. Every well executed tactic is an opportunity to grow your business.

16.   Create a marketing plan

17.   Create a sales plan

18.   Learn a new marketing tactic.

19.   Call two more potential customers.

20.   Call your existing customers and thank them for their business.

21.   Write and submit a proposal to a new client.

22.   Write and submit a press release that pegs a newsworthy item to your company's activities.

23.   Host a lunch, happy hour, or party at your offices.

Use Marketing Words That Have Juice!

Note: My children were pre-teens when I owned my business. They would surprise me with their creativity!

My son made up another word today...blurvy. It's a cross between blurry and wavy. Here's how he used it. "Mom, your voice on your Bluetooth sounds blurvy." After arguing that blurvy was not a word, I decided to just go with it.

He and his sister have either made up or introduced me to many interesting words that may someday make it into the lexicon. Words like:

- Ginormous- pronounced (Ji-nor-mus) (a cross between gigantic and enormous.)
- Jank- meaning disgusting or of bad quality
- Blurvy- (see above)
- Soupy- not a new word but used in a new way...as in I don't like books that are too soupy (full of extra words)

All of these words could be used with a great deal of confidence in the marketing realm because they are descriptive and full of 'juice.' One of the hallmarks of good marketing is to use a fresh approach. Words are an important part of that fresh approach. There are marketing words that are just tired. Words like "good," the "best," "qualified," and the "right choice." These words have no "juice" or zest or verve. What new words could you use?

24. Identify two juicy words to describe your firm's value.

Branding! Be Consistent

Small business owners are too busy bringing in work, managing business, and balancing the books to worry about consistent application of their branding and graphic presence.

I urge you to MAKE TIME! Often, we see logos and other branding elements that appear like a sweater that is faded, stretched out and snagged. Branding adds value to your company. But, it must be consistently applied. If you decide to have your logo redesigned, request that your design firm provides not only design files consisting of .jpgs and .eps or vector files but also a style guide that clearly explains how to use the logo or graphic design in multiple applications.

The PMS/Pantone colors, CMYK, RGB, and Hex colors should be outlined and identified. The fonts, the taglines, and the appropriate use of the logo in print and web should be explained. Ideally, your graphic design firm would provide you with all the details clearly explained for any possible use including letterhead, email marketing, social media (Facebook, LinkedIn, Twitter), email signature lines, brochures, websites, blogs, etc. Then, use the guide to apply your logo consistently and often!

25. **Create a style guide for your logo and brand.**

Marketing Strategy is More Important than Social Networking!

An Arizona Republic's article during 2009 was, "Fizzling arts fundraiser offers lessons." It discussed the less than overwhelming response of the "MyArtsCommunity.org" campaign. As the article aptly pointed out, there were several errors and problems that plagued the campaign. They pinpointed timing as the primary culprit. Not enough time and bad timing, specifically, were identified as the issues that made this campaign's ROI (-349%)! (They earned $22,258 but spent $100,000.) Timing was one of the issues but the two bigger issues were ill-considered marketing strategy and a lack of compelling messaging.

First, let's examine the messaging. "I perform for you, now it's your turn" is a guilt-laden message for people who have already spent money to see the performance happen. People spending money to see a performance have exchanged money for entertainment. They do not have residual guilt that they underpaid or that they were offered a "favor" by the artists. Most arts advocates (of which I am one) realize that the cost of tickets does not come close to covering the cost of performing or launching an exhibition, but the public at large is not aware of the underlying arts operations issues of small community arts groups. The public are more educated about mega stars who are living a life of luxury. When the ticket prices to an "artistic" event are similar to a rock or pop concert, they may not realize the difference in economic models between the two. So, perhaps, a better approach should have been to educate the public about the fact that their ticket only pays for 30% of the performance cost and then, offer the call to action. But make that call to action positive, like "Thanks for making it possible for me to continue performing for you."

Second, the tools were given more consideration than the strategy. Yes, social media is smart. Yes, it reaches a new generation of supporters who haven't traditionally supported the arts. But, the reality is that the traditional donors don't embrace new media. The "over 50 crowd" who has the means and interest to invest in the arts is still a face to face, read it in the newspaper or in a letter kind of group. Growing a new support base among the millennials is ABSOLUTELY CRITICAL to the future of the arts. No question about it! However, this will not be accomplished in six weeks. The millennials have the potential to be GREAT supporters of the arts but a long-term education process needs to be instigated and installed in their culture. And, hold on to your hats, Boomers, it may involve more technology, and a new way of performing, presenting, and experiencing the arts.

I wish the MyArtsCommunity.org campaign had been more successful. We need to support the arts. However, like many marketing campaigns that ignore the fundamentals like strategy and messaging, the chance of success is greatly reduced. Marketing tools do not and cannot supersede marketing fundamentals.

26.   Know your ideal client demographic.

Authentic Marketing

I have been marketing or selling for more than 20 years. I now own a marketing firm that provides marketing strategy and tools to all types of businesses. I am working extensively with some of the digital marketing tools like search engine optimization, social networking, blogging, websites, email marketing, etc.

What keeps coming to mind is that THE most important aspect of marketing is the importance of authenticity. It is easy to shift your focus from the customer to the new techniques. It can be somewhat addictive to learn about and then focus on tools and techniques that will drive website traffic or increase your links or create a "buzz" or go "viral."

Yet through my years of selling, whether it is face to face sales, online marketing, or advertising, the most important tenet is that of authenticity. It is critical to understand who you are, who your client is, and then, deliver a message that compels or persuades the client to act.

Yes, it is tempting to stand up in meetings and talk about SEO and blogging and other terms that non-technical people find "scary." And, it is important to understand those tools but the fundamentals; strategy, measurement, creativity, and authenticity are still the most critical aspects of marketing today.

27.   Write one authentic statement about your business.

Marketing Strategies to Open New Markets

Recently a client asked me how best to move into a new market and increase his chances to be successful at the lowest cost. I thought about this dilemma and as we discussed the options it occurred to me that there were about six key strategies to employ.

They are:

- Be creative and edgy.
- Focus on key potential clients.
- Have personal interaction.
- Repetition.
- Messaging from multiple sources.
- Keep track of your results.

Implement these key marketing strategies and you will realize marketing results quickly.

Marketing Whimsy

"If the circus is coming to town....

And you paint a sign saying 'Circus Coming to the Fairground Saturday,' that's advertising.

If you put the sign on the back of an elephant and walk him into town, that's promotion.

If the elephant walks through the mayor's flowerbed, that's publicity.

If you can get the mayor to laugh about it, that's public relations.

And if you planned the elephant's walk, that's marketing."

Source: Reader's Digest

What to Expect From a Marketing Firm or Advertising Agency (And What We Expect From Our Clients)

I wrote this article after nearly two years of owning a marketing firm / advertising agency.

I have written a "guide" for small businesses or individuals that are considering hiring an advertising agency. The guide specifies what a business can count on from a marketing firm and what the marketing firm or advertising agency needs its clients to know.

You can count on us to:

1.   Provide you with very high quality work in formats you can use in the specified print or web formats. We will provide the appropriate files to the printer, web developer, or publisher to ensure your project is completed according to the requirements. Our goal is to do it right the first time in as seamless, timely manner as possible.

2.   Follow through and complete your project in a timely and professional manner. We will adhere to deadlines, incorporate your changes and accommodate you!

3.   All communications will be courteous, professional, and friendly. Our goal is to make your life easier!

4.   Go that extra mile to ensure you are a "raving fan." We will be looking for ways to add value to your business.

5.   Communicate the status of your project on a weekly or bi-weekly basis. No one likes surprises.

6.   Advise you of any changes to the project scope and any additional charges that may apply.

7. Have the right professionals available to you when you need or want them. Whether they are staff, consultants or outside vendors, each provider has been carefully selected because of the service and quality they provide.

8. Accurate and timely billing for your projects. No surprises!

9. Expertise in marketing, writing, graphic design, advertising, photography, and strategy. We are professionals. You deserve professional service.

10. Exceptional quality, the highest level of service, and clear communications!

We count on you to know:

1.   All of our projects are priced based on time. We provide an informed estimate as to the time involved to complete your project in a timely and high quality manner. Our goal is to provide a quality project that adds value to your business. We do not cut corners nor do we linger.

2.   We want to invest in your business, be your partner as you grow and add value by going "above and beyond." However, know that most times when you pick up the phone to call us there will be a charge. No matter how friendly the call or no matter how long we "chat", like a lawyer our time is money and we do charge for it.

3.   Read the scope carefully. Any adjustments made to scope will be charged in addition to the original project fee. For example, if you decide to create a multi-page brochure instead of a postcard there will be additional charges. Additionally, if you change your mind, decide your business is moving in another direction, or decide your niece / nephew / neighbor / assistant can complete the project, you are required to pay (according to our contract) for the work completed.

4.   If you are not sure what you want, let us know! We will provide you with an estimate to "scope" your project. If you choose to pay us to scope your project, we will give you

the files, site maps, and/or parameters we used which will allow you to take the scope to any marketing firm so you can price the project with multiple professionals. If you choose to award MTG with the project, we will likely give you credit for the scope.

5. Our prices are determined by the quality of our work, market rates, value of the project to your business, time involved, and our costs. You can find marketing services for less money and you can find them for quite a bit more. If you have any concerns about rates, please discuss them prior to the project beginning.

6. We often interface with vendor/partners (i.e. photographers, printers, publishers, video vendors, software developers) on your behalf. We have contractual arrangements with those vendors. These contracts are primarily in writing, although sometimes are oral agreements. When you sign a contract with MTG, you are agreeing to pay us so we can pay our partners. If you change your mind, we still need to pay those vendors. Therefore, contractually, you still need to pay us for work completed.

7. In this digital age, there are a number of ways to complete a marketing project. You can handle nearly every bit of marketing yourself with the programs and internet

services available to you. If you handle it yourself, it will be less expensive than hiring professionals. When you hire an agency, you are hiring people who have invested in marketing, writing, photography, graphic design and business development as their profession. Like other professionals we constantly stay abreast of current trends, we are informed by many years of experience in our field, we have special training and/or education and we work in the field EVERY day. Hiring an agency is an investment. Like your lawyer, stylist, accountant, or housekeeper, we are service providers. Please decide if you truly want to invest in a professional or if you would prefer to save the money and do it yourself. We have a "do it yourself" section on our website to assist you with providers we recommend.

8. Please communicate your goals for dates of completion, important milestones, and expectations explicitly and up front. We can then determine if we can meet your goals. If not, we will provide referrals to other agencies. If so, you can count on us to meet your goals!

9. Every project will require some involvement from you. No one knows your business like you do. Although we will research your business, write and design from our knowledge base and extrapolate as much as possible from

your existing materials, we will need you to provide content for your website, advertisement, proposal, or brochure. Then, we count on you to read and review what we provide. If you "sign off" on the project or content, we will assume you have read it.

10. Although we LOVE our clients, we are in business to pay our mortgages and feed our kids just like you. Our business is not a hobby, an extracurricular activity, or an interim compromise while we wait for the economy to turn around. Our goal is to create a long-term mutually beneficial relationship. We look forward to creating a relationship with you that benefits both of us!

Why Should You Use A Marketing Firm Or Advertising Agency?

Most business owners and professionals are savvy enough to understand the importance of having a website, direct mail campaign (postcards) or a brochure. With the proliferation of online marketing firms, it can be tempting to buy your website, brochure or postcard quickly and without marketing strategy or marketing planning. It is a good feeling to take charge and quickly solve those pesky or overwhelming marketing problems. However, I urge you to consider hiring a firm, if only just to develop a core strategy.

Not starting out with a marketing strategy and instead starting with marketing tools, like collateral, websites, or postcards, wastes your time and money. It is akin to going to the grocery store when you are hungry, buying everything that looks good to you, taking it home and trying to cook several nutritious tasty meals from your chosen ingredients of vanilla ice cream, bread, chicken fingers, and olives.

By giving into the temptation of putting up a website via a template or developing a brochure from an online source, you are missing the most important steps. These steps are:

- Deciding your buyer profiles and determining how your buyers communicate and buy.
- Determining who you are (branding.)
- Setting marketing goals.
- And, then setting a communication, visual, and tactical strategy to connect with your potential clients and move them in the direction of buying your services or products.

Without this critical strategic marketing planning, you may as well mail all of your potential clients $5-100 dollars (the amount that your collateral, website, and search engine optimization will cost) and never follow up.

There is definitely a place for online marketing firms that provide tools only. You want a brochure, you got it. You want a logo, you got it. But, unless you have the right marketing message for the targeted audience and deliver it in a way they understand and appreciate, you may regret the speed and ease at which you decide to "solve" your marketing problems.

28.   Create buyer profiles

29.   Discover how your buyers communicate and buy.

30.   Decide who you are

31.   Set marketing goals.

32.   Create a communication plan

Experience at the Taco Shop

Recently, I visited a taco shop in Phoenix that was written up in the newspaper. I rarely read the newspaper anymore (like most people if you look at the numbers) but I had grabbed the newspaper on my way out to a (rare for me) leisurely breakfast.

In the local section of the newspaper was a glowing restaurant review of a new "gourmet taco shop." The review was written so well and the author of the article was so impressed with the restaurant that my mouth watered while reading the article.

Later that day we decided to give the restaurant a try. What I found there was interesting. First, the restaurant was clearly not prepared for the publicity. They only had three people working. It was set up as a self-service restaurant, sort of. You went up to the counter to order the food (which was very good, by the way.) The salsa bar was also self-service. Yet, there were no garbage cans, nor were you able to refill your drinks yourself, nor was there a way to get more chips....you get the picture. The three employees were polite and hustled but was it really fair to them to have a line of fifteen people out the door and no way to serve them successfully. I'm sure they felt just as uncomfortable as all the patrons that had to stack their rack on one of the tables because there was no place to put your trash.

The second and interesting observation was that as I sat there and ate my yummy food, newspaper demographics became very clear. Nearly every person that showed up at the door of the restaurant (not including me) was over the age of 60, all of them citing the newspaper article.

The moral of the story is two-fold. First, if you know you are going to get press coverage, work out the kinks BEFORE you get the coverage. Second, newspaper advertising and editorial is lost on the young. The generation that reads newspapers is aging and will be lost in 10-20 years. Either view them as a niche marketing vehicle or reconfigure them so that they are compelling for the young.

33.   Create a list of the marketing tactics you are currently using.

34.   Ask yourself, do they reach my ideal customer?

Marketing to the Government

I have recently embarked upon the curious and interesting world of federal procurement. There are a few things I have learned that may help others looking to follow the same path.

- Identify the agency, departments or areas of government that are the best fit for your organization's offerings.
- Look for procurement shows that may have attendees from those agencies or departments. By attending a trade show, you can see a number of government representatives who are very helpful and knowledgeable.
- Register with CCR. (HINT: Get a DUNS # first.)
- Register with FedBizOpps.
- Register with ORCA.
- Prepare a qualification statement
- When you see a relevant project, prepare a professional and persuasive proposal that will present your firm in the best possible light.
- Continue to market yourself to the targeted agencies.
- Get on the GSA schedule for your NAICS code.
- If you fall into a special category, like minority, woman, or veteran owned business, obtain certification.

Strategies for Marketing to the Government

Because we respond to government proposals (like RFPs and RFQs) I am often asked about how to acquire government business. The simple answer is: it requires a marketing strategy just like any market sector. However, it also requires some special marketing knowledge and sensitivity to the government procurement process.

When deciding to add government as a market sector to pursue, the first decision is the type of government entity you want to pursue? Municipalities, counties, states, universities, and the federal government all require different marketing strategies, have different rules, may require different levels of marketing investment.

City and county governments are usually more approachable and the procurement process is more straightforward. Also, many states incorporate a preference for businesses in their jurisdiction. Typically, the city, county and state government managers are often very accessible and will be open to developing a professional business relationship. Below are eight basic steps to take to begin approaching marketing to local government entities.

1. To begin, determine the two-three entities and/or agencies that you would like to pursue.

2. Before a request for proposal is issued, meet with the "end users" (i.e. the people needing your products or services) and then meet with procurement.

3. You may even want to attend some pre-proposal meetings where you are not likely to propose so you can get a sense of the way the entity does business.

4. Complete any special certifications or registrations that are required. For example, the City of Phoenix requires companies register and are issued an affirmative action certificate.

5. Using the Freedom of Information Act (FOIA) or the Public Records Laws for your state, take the time to review responses to the Request for Proposals previously issued.

6. Then, begin the process of writing a proposal for your company. Begin to develop resumes, a company description, and other key information that will be included in a request for qualifications or request for proposal.

7. Wait for the release of the RFP/RFQ and then, write a response to the RFP that is persuasive, responsive, and creative.

8. Whether you win or lose, request a debrief with the procurement officer.

It is a cumbersome process but once you get initiated you will learn that it's just another approach to business and it is very rewarding, especially when you
develop relationships with the people that work for the government.

40.   Submit a request for proposal.

41.   Request a debrief after the contract is awarded.

Collateral Materials (Print) in 3D!

There are two trends on a potentially positive collision course. Is it just me or for a time were most movies produced in Hollywood presented in 3D? Also, having heard over and over again print materials, brochures, and collateral materials are dead, I found that it was not quite true. When these two trends clashed, they made... ouila', pop-ups!

We had been searching for interesting print materials to take our clients' marketing messages to the next level. After some extensive research, we found a couple of terrific resources. Pop-up Mailers, located in the UK, recently sent us a terrific grab bag of samples that are fun, exciting, surprising, and attention-grabbing. When I opened the box, large and small items started popping up all over. Special sliding cards have movement. Some of the boxes include a place to contribute to a charity. These are innovative examples of collateral materials that are effective because they garner attention and interest.

The other resource is located in Massachusetts, Graphic Sales Products. Their samples weren't quite as attention-grabbing but were more highly customized. The samples included boxes, folders, 3-D glasses paired with 3-D graphics and other materials that can be well-integrated with an overall campaign.

Think out-of-the-box, be creative, and innovate!

42.   Explore new and different print strategies.

Marketing Strategy: Awards

There are a number of wonderful awards that are available for small, medium and even large businesses. By applying for and winning awards, you gain a number of distinct benefits.

First, the exercise of applying for awards provides you with the opportunity to hone your value proposition, frame and/or crystallize your key growth strategies and position yourself in a market of award winners.

Second, you gain the visibility and exposure to the business community and organization that is offering the award.

Third, it gives you the ability to gain a new skill set, namely that of interviewing and speaking about the culture and purpose of your company.

43. **Identify awards that you can pursue.**

44. **Submit applications to at least one of them.**

Should you develop a blog or create a website?

One of the options for the cash strapped person who is looking to develop a website or create a web presence is to create a blog. There are both positive and negative considerations when making the decision to create a blog (especially if you are publishing a blog instead of developing a website.)

A freestanding blog is a free or inexpensive way to develop a web presence. The word "blog" sounds "techie" but really, a blog is nothing more than a notebook online for you to write about your service or product, thoughts or opinions, much like you would write a letter and post it on a bulletin board. If you know how to use WORD, you know how to write a blog.

Who should consider a blog? Creating a blog is perfect for someone who has limited cash (the cost is free or nominal,) would like to create a web presence, and is committed to updating the blog content regularly. Be prepared for a community to develop around your writing. The more compelling your text, the more subscribers you will attract.

Reasons to choose a freestanding blog: It's free! It's easy. It's a way to stick your "toe" into the web waters. You can literally create a blog in 1 minute. The "best" sites to develop your blog are <u>Wordpress</u>, <u>Blogger</u>, <u>TumblR</u>, Weebly, Wix, Medium, SquareSpace, and others.

Why wouldn't you choose a freestanding blog? A website is a better choice if you are launching a business or have an established business. A website, at this time, is much more robust. The best choice is to create a website with a blog embedded in it. Why? Integrating a blog in your website allows you to reap the rewards of keyword rich text in all blog posts. A freestanding blog will not provide the best search engine optimization. It is more ideal to create your own URL. Blogs aren't searched nearly as often as websites, although organic searches will often pull blog sites. Also, there are limitations to customizing and branding a freestanding blog.

45. Create a blog.

46. Weave key words into the content.

Web Site Marketing: The Top Places To Register Your Company on the Web

Most people over 40 years old remember that everyone used the Yellow Pages and only the Yellow Pages to list their company's phone number and address. Now, there are so many places to register your business it can be quite confusing. Here are the top places where your business should be listed on the web (and most of them are FREE)!

Google Local Business

Even if it can't find your website, if you use the Google Directory feature, people will be able to find you. This is the local business listing site for Google. You can add your address and mapped location for free.

Yahoo Local Business

Bing

Yelp

Merchant Circle

White Pages

Super Pages

Yellow Book

Yellow Bot

Manta

CitySearch

MapQuest

Hotfrog

Kudzu

Local.com

Directory Critic

Foursquare

Dex Knows

Best of the Web

Live Search (aka Microsoft)

Yellow Pages

Don't be confused with Yellow Book. Yellow Pages have much better traffic and are ranked significantly higher than the Yellow Book.

This exercise takes about 1 hour (less than that if you already have the copy about describing your business.) I highly recommend you do it. Then, people will be able to find you no matter where they look.

47. **List your company with Google Local Business, Yahoo Local Business, and the Yellow Pages.**

The Top Five Techniques and Tools for Website Promotion and Website Marketing

Search Optimization is a moving but important target for website marketing, website promotion and to increase web traffic, yet quality of content is more important than SEO for SEO's sake.

Search Engine Optimization (SEO) (or search optimization or web site marketing) is the most important aspect of website design and development IF you are relying on search optimization to provide you with leads and customers. Yet, SEO remains an elusive goal. Ideally, SEO will position your business on page one of Google, Yahoo, and Bing as people search the key word that relates to your business. Ideally, this optimization will be of little or no cost to you. The ideal is a good goal but it's better to shoot for the "best possible ranking."

Although Google is very egalitarian, there is still a benefit to those who pay SEO companies to increase web traffic by enhancing links, focusing on key words, blogging, creating PPC campaigns, and writing keyword rich content. There are a number of ways to enhance your ranking but it's no mystery (if you are prepared to read many books and web articles.)

The best way to increase web traffic via website marketing is to touch your website (i.e. update its content) regularly. Whether you tackle website promotion by writing a blog or update content regularly with a content management program, do update your website with relevant content routinely and regularly. This practice will not only increase web traffic but also allow for search optimization and website promotion.

Second, do a keyword search assessment or hire someone to do a keyword search assessment in order to generate Meta source code and keyword rich content. When people search key words, your website will appear.

Third, for relevant website marketing, to increase web traffic, and for search optimization, build links with companies that are complementary to yours.

Fourth, for search optimization pay attention to your H1, H2, H3, H4 title tags. Ensure they are keyword rich so when people search keyword your website appears.

Fifth, register your site with all of the major engines to ensure you are "listed." This technique is an often overlooked but critical part of website promotion and website marketing.

Those five steps alone will increase web traffic and raise your rankings above your competitors. For search optimization and to increase web traffic, completing these five steps will help.

48.   Explore Search Engine Optimization

Why Web Analytics Made Me Want to Keep Blogging

I didn't think anyone was reading my blog. There were few comments and the Google analytics weren't picking up the clicks. So, I got discouraged. But then...

I received a different analytics report that said I have had 5000 visitors to my blog in the last three months. WOW! That certainly changed my perception about the value of my blog and whether or not it was worth my time.

Web analytics are interesting. Increasingly, more people are aware they exist but often either don't check them or attribute meaning to them. However, they DO shift perceptions. I was recently speaking with Pam Slim, author of Escape from Cubicle Nation. She mentioned that book publishers actually want to know how many people currently read your blog before they will even consider publishing your book. To me that says if you want to publish you must blog AND track your numbers. Analytics help you do achieve that goal.

Web analytics also help you track conversions. If your web traffic is high but few people are buying, whether that means picking up the phone and ordering or clicking to purchase a product, there is a problem. Focus on improving website conversions and you will be better able to justify the website expense.

We recently rolled out a new program where we track web analytics and tie different campaigns to unique telephone numbers. Wouldn't it be nice to know which marketing tool generated the most sales? We now have a way to track this.

I could go on and on about the benefits of analytics but you get the idea. More data means more knowledge. More knowledge means better decisions about your business. So, in short, get GOOGLE analytics on your website and view them often! If you host on Go Daddy or other web hosts, often they have their own unique web analytics. Explore them!

49. Install Google Analytics on your website.

E-marketing: What Is It and How Will It Affect My Business?

Blogging, RSS Feeds, search engine optimization, and website analytics. What are they? And how do they affect you and your professional service firm? The following is the first in a three-part series about eMarketing. The first article will discuss websites, blogging, search engine optimization and the internet in general. Future articles will discuss email marketing, social networking, and other tools. Let's get started.

Recently, one of my clients told me that he wasn't convinced that his website and certainly any other eMarketing tools were important to his engineering firm. He did not believe in their value, had spent thousands over the years on the website, and he certainly wasn't going to invest one more dollar on refreshing them. His point was that because the construction business is so collaborative and relationship-oriented, the website seems like a "nice to have."

While I can sympathize with his frustration, I don't agree with him. The present and the future focus of communications will be electronic. Do you want proof? The postal service is considering dropping service to five days per week. Newspapers around the country are bankrupt or changing their delivery formats. More and more news, music, mail, and marketing are being delivered electronically. That said, not every electronic media innovation may be for you or your firm but a website that is strategically designed and updated regularly is essential. In fact, most people do not realize how important their website is because they never get their web traffic reports. They do not realize how many people are going to their website to review their projects and services before they pick up the phone to make the call and inquire about their services. As a former director of marketing for several architecture firms, we often made decisions about which engineers to select for teams based on our knowledge COMBINED with the projects we found on the various engineers' websites. The developers that contacted us mentioned that they had found us or qualified us based on our website projects. So those firms that have dated websites are doing themselves a disservice.

There are three key reasons (from a marketing perspective) in a business to business setting that people use the internet. Those are to research, search and buy. For many professional service firms, especially those that serve exclusively other businesses, the research aspect is more important than the "search" or "buy" aspects. No electronic media will ever replace the value of personal relationships and networking. However, the website significantly augments those efforts. For example, suppose you have spent hours, weeks, or months on business development. When the time comes, you want to know that when they visit your website or forward it to a colleague, it accurately represents your firm and persuasively communicates the reason they should hire you. Clients and potential clients do their "research" by visiting your **website.**

The "search" aspect of the internet is important to firms (especially consumer-oriented) where their prospective clients don't know their web address. They just want to find an excellent attorney/accountant/dog sitter, etc. If you are a consumer-oriented firm, or you don't have a significant business development effort, **search engine optimization (SEO)** is a must. In short, SEO is the group of techniques that are used to promote and rank your site with the search engines (like Google, Yahoo, MSN, Ask!) So, when someone searches for "structural engineer Tucson," if you are search engine optimized, you will be pulled up on the first page or two on the search engine on which you are optimized.

So what should you do?

- Take a look at your website (you'd be amazed how many people never look at their sites!)

- Visit your competitor's websites.

- Then, decide your goals for the website. Is it to persuade people to call you for more information? Is it to answer clients' easy questions? Is it to gather resumes? Is it to proactively or reactively market your firm? Do you want a place to communicate with clients online?

- Objectively ask yourself if your website meets your goals. Does it have the functionality you want? Is the content compelling, accurate, and current? Does it reflect your company's culture?

- Next, ask your IT person or whoever hosts your site to provide web traffic reports. Those reports will provide information like how many people visit your site, where they are visiting from, the pages they viewed and how long they stayed on the site.

- If you decide you need a refresh, talk to a professional (not a friend's kid who just graduated from college) about your goals for the website. Make sure the person you hire understands not only web development or design but also marketing and how the website fits into your overall marketing message and plan. Investigate search engine optimization (the various techniques that are used to ensure your website is found on the web,) key words (words people use to find you on the web, if they don't already have your web address), and the impact of various decisions on your overall goals. (E.g. if you are interested in search engines finding you, don't develop your site in flash.)

The word **blog** is short for "web log." It is a way for you to update your website, add some dialogue and engage in conversation with your website viewers. Blogging has become extremely important in the world of politics, journalism and search engine optimization. Because blogging is almost instantaneous publishing to the world, in any industry where information is critical, and speed matters blogging can move opinion and seed more traditional journalistic publications. For search engine optimization, when websites are updated frequently, they are more likely to get higher page rankings, meaning they are more likely to be optimized. If you want to find the latest information, and you have found a blog that you really like, you can register for a **Real Simple Syndication (RSS) Feed**. A RSS Feed is essentially a subscription to the blog. When new updates are posted, you either receive the post or a notice that a new post is available for you to read.

The last part of the website information you should be aware is the importance of **website analytics.** Every marketer needs to have an understanding of where your web traffic comes from, who visits, when they visit, where they spend most of their time, and how they found you (i.e. which search engine, directly typing in your address, etc.) Every good marketer should request web analytic reports, understand them, and use the information to improve the website.

All of the previous concepts, the website, analytics, blogging, SEO are all related to people finding you. Next article we will discuss you driving people to you as we discuss email marketing.

50. **Conduct a review of your digital marketing strategies. Are they meeting your objectives? Do they generate leads?**

Website Marketing: The Top Five Measures For Your Website Page Rank

Using your website as a source of leads and business intelligence requires a strategy. Search engine optimization (getting your web page ranked on Google) and turning your website from a brochure into a viable business tool requires that you benchmark how you "rank" compared to your competitors.

There are a number of free tools that you can use to assess how your website measures up to your competitors. Here are the top five:

www.alexa.com

This site will give your page rank and your competitors' page rank.

www.google.com

Google is not just for searching! If you download the google tool bar, it will allow you to measure the page rank of the web pages you visit, including your own.

www.websitegrader.com

Hubspot is a terrific site for assessing the effectiveness of your search engine optimization.

www.seomoz.org/trifecta

SEOMOZ is another site that provides a free page rank tool to give you another perspective.

As a bonus, if you want to investigate your Firefox ranking, you may check:

http://tools.seobook.com/firefox/rank-checker/

Once you understand your starting point, you will be able to begin to improve your web traffic and/or your page rank and optimization.

51.   Register your site on these website ranking websites.

Social networking: The basics!

Social networking is the new way to broaden your network and stay connected. Also, businesses can use it to recruit, manage the perception of their company image, and market their products of services. For individuals, most of the sites have discussion groups and group like-minded participants. All of these sites are FREE to join. Below is a summary of the big four (LinkedIn, Instagram, Facebook, and Twitter) most popular social networking sites:

LinkedIn: With 530 million participants, everyone should be linked in. It is ranked as the 30th most popular website in the world. It has a disproportionately high amount of graduate school graduates and the average age of the users is between 25 and 44. This site connects you to friends, but more importantly, to prospective clients and business opportunities. This is a business site.

Instagram: With 800 million participants, most businesses could benefit from Instagram. It is ranked as the 17th most popular website in the world. It has a disproportionately high amount of female users (68%).

Facebook: More social, less professional. Facebook is the 3rd most popular website in the world, as ranked by web traffic. Users have some college education and are typically female.

Twitter: the 13th most popular site, the average user is male, and has college or graduate students. This is primarily a business site with social usage, as well. (Especially popular with celebrities, reporters, and notable persons.)

Tumblr With 30-50 million participants, business should consider using Tumblr. It is ranked as the 55th most popular website in the world. It has an equal number of female and male users. This is both a personal and business site.

Pinterest With 150 million participants, especially retail and product sites should use Pinterest. It is ranked as the 77th most popular website in the world. It has a disproportionately high amount of female users. This is a personal and business site.

52. Open a personal LinkedIn account.

53. Create a company page on Facebook.

The Importance of a Content Management System for Your Website

When businesses purchase a website, they often put themselves completely in the hands of the web developer. They rely on that web developer to provide them with the best website that suits their web marketing needs. I have found that many businesses are not served well by their web developers.

"Old school" web developers reveled in being "proprietary." They loved the fact that they had knowledge and a vocabulary that befuddled people. There was a certain satisfaction when they used words that even the most intelligent person didn't understand unless they were active in the web development area. So, for most people, a website was something that they "put up" and rarely touched again. Going back to the web developer to make changes was costly and the process somewhat mysterious. In fact, I believe that part of the skyrocketing success of social networking is that anyone can update their content, anytime. There are no special skills required.

One way to control website costs and control your website content is to employ a content management system (an editing tool that allows them to update their site without hiring a web developer.) The tool adds cost to the beginning of the project but it more than pays for itself by the time a few edits are performed by you instead of paying the web developer. And, insist that the web developer teach you how to use the tool. For example, I knew how to edit content but not "hide" a page on my site. I asked my developer to "hide" the page and then I decided to edit the content and "reveal" it again. I was charged $22 to hide it and then $22 to reveal it. It took the developer about 1 second to check the box that is required to hide a page. $44 isn't a whole lot of money but I would have rather spent it on something other than having someone check a box on a page.

Updating your website should be as simple as writing an email. And, it can be. Insist that you add a content management system to your site and it will lessen your dependence on your web developer (allowing them to work on the more complex programming issues that they prefer to do, anyway.)

54. **Install a content management system or if you already have one, ensure at least one person updates the site, weekly.**

Social Media: Style versus substance

You know the person. They always look perfect, have the best of everything, and are always at the front of every classroom and at the top of every list. Now, we have social media that feeds their desperate search for respect and legitimacy, because these people are "Top Linked" or have more friends and followers than anyone else.

Social media, whether you are talking Twitter, Facebook, LinkedIn, or YouTube (and others) feeds a growing problem in our business world and society. People who believe style is more important than substance and quantity is more important than quality. People are using Social Media to trumpet to the world their legitimacy, as though numbers alone tell the story. After all, if someone has 5000 twitter followers, people must really care about what they are doing, right? And, if someone has over 1000 links on LinkedIn, they must be really connected! Or, if someone has over 500 friends on Facebook, they must be popular.

Search Engine Optimization has a similar problem. People are blogging and tweeting and linking for the sole purpose of driving up the rankings on search engines. Most of the time, once again, style (i.e. key words, length, activity) is more important than substance. But what happens when the visitor gets to the site? Shouldn't there be substantial content to reward them for their efforts?

I have begun to develop my own "rules" about the social media, blogging, and SEO activity to fight this trend towards style over substance. I only...

1) "LinkIn" with people whom I have met (or with whom I have had prolonged long distance contact.) And, I only post business-related news.

2) Facebook with people with whom I have had regular and prolonged in-person contact, i.e. the people who I care about what they do every day. In fact, I am in the process of unfriending people on Facebook so that I can accomplish this.

3) Blog with observations, lessons, or rants/raves. I don't sit down with the keyword list and generate blog posts from that list to improve SEO.

4) Write press releases when I want to announce something. We don't generate them to drive SEO.

5) Follow twitter to monitor trends and the press. It's really not important what my dogs ate for dinner! I don't think most people care.

6) Consider all of these mediums as tools. They are not the ultimate measure of me or my company's legitimacy or popularity.

So, instead of being intimidated or feeling bad because I don't have 4000 LinkedIn connections or 1000 friends or 5000 followers, I am taking a stand for quality over quantity, substance over style! What about you?

55. **Proactively decide your approach to social media. How often do you want to post? What will the content be?**

The Top 10+ 'Secrets' of Google

Most people when asked about Google know it's a search engine. After all, to "Google" something has become a verb in our lexicon. Most people know Google as the clean white search box they see when they visit www.Google.com.

If people are really pressed they may also mention that Google has email (Gmail) and maps (Google maps.) What people don't know is that there is a much bigger "beyond the search" part of Google. In fact, Google has a patent search function, video calling, messaging, scholarly paper research, a book search feature, and translation services. Those are just a few of the many services that Google offers. To discover these areas, sign in to your Google account (Gmail is easiest) and then click on "My Account." You will see an area that mentions "personal settings" and then another area that says "My products." The "My products" area shows you the Google services you are already using. However, to discover more, click on "Try something new." In that area you will discover 77 additional Google services. The ten most interesting, include:

Allo

Android Pay

Duo

Google Express

Google Trips

Patent Search

Scholarly Paper Research

Earth (see the ocean floor and more!)

Books (search text of books)

Translate websites into another language

Trends

Google Digital Garage

Have fun!

56. Get to know Google.

Need A Website? Six Things to Consider When Hiring a Web Developer

Routinely, people promise fantastic websites and yet do not deliver on their promises. Some of these people have the best of intentions, others do not. Developing a website seems easy but there are complexities and components most business owners may not realize exist. Below is a primer and questions to ask your web developer.

The six critical components of website design and development are:

1) Strategy: How does this website connect with new and existing clients? What is the purpose of the site? What are the goals of the site?

YOU PROBABLY WANT: Someone who can understand your goals and can connect the website to your business or marketing strategy. Someone who understands website is a critical business tool. Someone who understands ROI, web analytics and measurement.

2) Design: Who is going to design the site? How many versions will I get to choose from?

YOU PROBABLY WANT: 2-3 (More than 1)

3) Content: Who is going to write the copy? Do you need to provide them with materials or are they going to write it? What about photos? Do you need to provide those or do they use stock photography? If so, who owns the content of the site? Do you own the copyright or do they?

YOU PROBABLY WANT: The copywriting to be a blend of you providing information and them writing for you in a web friendly (keyword friendly way) way. Make sure they can WRITE! You need to own the copyright as soon as you pay for the site called, work-for-hire.

4) Development (or coding): Who codes the site? What language are they using? (HTML, PHP, CSS are the most common.) Is a content management system going to be incorporated so that you can make your own changes to the site? If so, how much will it cost?

YOU PROBABLY WANT: PHP or HTML because they are open source. And, you want a content management system if it's not too costly. WordPress works.

5) Project Management: Who is going to pull all this together? Is it you (the client), the web developer or someone else?

YOU PROBABLY WANT: They should do it. The project management should start from the beginning with a defined site map. You should have a clear understanding of the end result.

6) Search Engine Optimization (SEO): Is the site going to be created so it is SEO friendly? What SEO practices are you going to employ in order to make sure your website can get "found" on the web (especially in Google.)

YOU PROBABLY WANT: Require clear and understandable language. If your web developer provides vague or confusing answers, ask them to explain it to you in language you can understand. There is NO reason for them to talk to you in "tech speak." Websites are not rocket science. They just are a specialized area of expertise. When you talk to your accountant or lawyer you want to understand them. It is exactly the same with a web developer or marketing professional.

57. Refresh your website.

Using Avatars on your Website

Avatars are in our future! What is an avatar? According to dictionary.com, 1) in *Hindu Mythology it is* the descent of a deity to the earth in an incarnate form or some manifest shape; the incarnation of a god; 2) an embodiment or personification, as of a principle, attitude, or view of life. But on the internet, an avatar is...

A graphical image that represents a person. There is currently a terrific site for Avatars (www.sitepal.com) that allows you to create your own avatar from existing choices or upload your own photo. It's affordable and my guess, a new trend in website design "must have's."

58.   Create an avatar.

Web analytics

There is a huge range of web adoption. I spent a considerable amount of time today on the telephone with someone who candidly admits that he never uses a computer but "should." And, at the same time, Mind the Gap offered web traffic, web analytics, and web reporting for our clients. The exciting aspect of marketing in the Web 2.0 world is the aspect of measurability. Finally, marketers can determine where the ROI is. Websites with analytics can provide information about how people are searching for you, what they are interested in on your site, how long they stay, how many people visit your site, where your visitors are coming from and which sites sent them there.

We review the web traffic and other reports for multiple clients and they tell us a great deal about web clients. Decisions can then be made about what to emphasize and what sells. Landing pages on one client's site will tell us what search engine optimization techniques are working, and what type of clients visit their website. Is it the family looking for a vacation, the motorcycle riders, or the business traveler that is the most motivated to go to the website and then "convert" to a paying client? With web analytics, we know! (Or, can at least make a good guess.)

The beauty of web analytics is that the market leader offers its product for free. Google Analytics is a user-friendly, clear package that can indicate to both beginners as well as more advanced marketing analysis the performance of your website.

If you haven't incorporate Google Analytics, or don't have a website, I encourage you to take a look.

59.   Review your web analytics.

Search Engine Optimization Assessment

How do you assess the performance of your search engine optimization? First, search google for the key word that you think people will use to search for you. Second, look at the source code (it can be found on your browser. Lastly, ask yourself the following questions:

What types of SEO efforts have been implemented?

- None, Light (Meta tags, page titles)
- Moderate (Blog, reciprocal linking etc.)
- Heavy (Multiple strategies in use)

What Keywords have you developed?

Do you have your key words in your Headers? Titles? Meta tags?

- Meta Tags, Alt Tags, Content

What internet directories are you listed with?

- *Google Yahoo! DMOZ Best of Web Other*
- *Have you submitted the site to Google Yahoo! Bing?*

Do you have a Blog?

Where is your blog?

What social networking sites do you frequent?

- Facebook, LinkedIn, Twitter, YouTube,

60. Identify five key words for your business.

61. Register with at least two internet directories.

Internet Marketing IDEAS to Try

Resolutions are ...well...typically forgotten or made to be broken, so, instead, let's call this year's list the five Marketing IDEAS to try.

1. Measure at least one of your marketing tools...like your website. Use Google Analytics to track your traffic. It's a small start but a good one.

2. If you already have accounts with the big three social media sites like Facebook, LinkedIn, and Twitter, try a new social media site. What about Instagram, ZoomInfo? Ryze? Give them a shot. If not, what are you waiting for...at a minimum get a LinkedIn account. It's critical for maintaining and growing your network of business relationships.

3. Ramp up your email marketing. At a minimum, start with Outlook. It's not the greatest tool but it can be done. (The secret is sending the emails out in small batches.)

4. Identify the key words people use to search for your type of business...and then apply them to your website. It sounds hard, but it's not. And, it is critical to being found on the web by people who don't know you.

5. Read a blog. You don't have to write one...yet. But, at least read one. Get rid of the fear of technology and dive in. It's fun, exciting, and will open your world to new possibilities.

62. **Measure your website analytics.**

63. **Try a new social media site.**

64. **Use email marketing.**

65. **Try a list swap with another firm.**

66. **Identify key words people use to search for your business.**

67. **Read a blog.**

Diversify your client base!

I remember a few years ago when my employer and I would make judgment calls about whether a potential opportunity was "worth the effort" to pursue. Times have changed!

Throughout my sales and marketing career there has always been a great deal of discussion about target markets, niche markets, and specializing. Every opportunity was evaluated from the perspective of "fit." Did it fit in our niche? Was it in a market sector that would strengthen our portfolio? Was the pursuit "worth it?" In fact, in my MBA program, this was one of the golden rules of marketing. No scatter shot marketing! Every marketing strategy should be carefully targeted.

I still believe this to be true. However, the net must be cast quite a bit broader than in the past. In fact, recently, I have encountered several experts that believe it is wise to not only cast your net wide but in several different bodies of water.

Because of the market uncertainties, we must view our marketing strategy like an investment portfolio. We must diversify between public and private sector clients. And, diversify among industries. AND, diversify our services. Like investing, our returns may be higher if we invest all of our time, energy, and money in one amazing growth stock, but the risk of that one stock yielding the highest returns is much, much higher than if we diversify among several that may generate high, erratic returns and low predictable returns.

So, while staying focused, evaluate your current client list and your target client list from the perspective of diversification.

68.   Choose one additional niche for your company to pursue.

Fear, Marketing, and Sales

Fear is an interesting thing. It stops us, guides us, and energizes us to do things that we may not normally do. It's surprising to me how many people turn to marketing because they are afraid of selling.

A sale is a fascinating process that involves initiating a relationship with someone you don't know or extending a relationship with someone you do. It is surprising to me how many people turn to marketing as a way to avoid selling. Yet, if they looked at sales not as a possibility of being rejected but as an opportunity to develop a new relationship, I'm wondering if they would be more eager to sell.

Somewhere along the way people have developed so many fears around selling. Yet, there is huge opportunity to develop as a person and a professional by overcoming that fear. Every time I'm about to take a risk, I feel some fear. The triumph is pushing through the fear and doing what I know is the right thing to do and what will ultimately result in success. Strength is built by overcoming fear. Overcoming the fear of sales will result in huge dividends for you, your business, and your life. So much of what we do every day is selling. Every time we convince someone to give us a discount, help us in a store, or introduce ourselves to someone, we are selling.

So, as one great author has said, "Feel the fear and do it anyway." Sales are an opportunity for people to know you and your products or services. They have a choice. If they choose no, it is not about you. It is NOTHING PERSONAL! So, use your marketing to support sales. Don't avoid sales. You can sell! Go for it!

69.   Pick up the phone or write a note to someone with whom you have always wanted to work. Be authentic. Ask for their business.

B2B vs. B2C What does it mean?

Mind the Gap identified itself as a business to business or B2B marketing firm. I realized the importance of this distinction when I hosted the vice president of a major consumer product company.

As I earnestly tried to explain that we used the product, were interested and indeed, ready, to provide package design support and marketing analytics, I realized that my pitch was falling on deaf ears. He was right! Although there is a growing convergence between B2C and B2B marketing, there is still a distinct difference. What is the difference? The sophistication of the buyer.

Typically, a B2B consumer is more sophisticated and somewhat removed from the purchase. After all, it isn't their money; it's their employers' money. They assess items from a detached viewpoint. They take pride in their ability to make shrewd decisions on behalf of their employers. Yet, the B2C consumer makes decisions from a more personal viewpoint. It is their cash, their hard earned money that they are spending. They want a lot for their purchases. They demand a lot from their purchases. And, rightly so!

I am no different. When I part with my hard earned dollars, I want to ensure that I buy quality. Other consumers may be buying something else. Regardless, I find consumers to be more whimsical and personal which is why I specialize in business to business marketing. I am much more likely to make a logical purchase for my business than for my personal life which is why I can better guess at the motivation of a business to business buyer.

70.   Determine if you are a B2B or B2C business.

71.   Does your marketing approach support your niche? Or, are you attempting to use B2C marketing approaches for a B2B firm?

Decide and Do

Yesterday I met with a prospective entrepreneur. She was terrific. Sharp, energetic, interesting, she wanted to discuss her path in the future. She was unsure of her direction. She was paralyzed by analysis.

Most entrepreneurs have an ability to view the future positively, live in possibility, and dream big. Their challenge is to focus. They need to decide what it is they want to do and execute with a vengeance. Although it is often more fun and less grueling to live in possibility, the hard work gets done and progress gets made when there is a relentless adherence to the plan...whether that plan is finishing a degree, executing a business plan, or realizing a life plan. Notice the thing in common...a plan. Although ideas are sexy and intoxicating because of the possibilities that they invoke, the success comes in the execution. Unless you are paid to dream and create ideas (what a cool job, if you are!), focusing is critical to achieving. Strategy and planning are sexy and fun. Executing is where the payoff is.

72. **Identify ONE thing to improve your marketing.**

73. **Do it.**

Technology as a Way to Establish Credibility

I have found myself recently in several uncomfortable situations. I worked with smart accomplished people with impressive resumes that were so technologically ignorant that it was clear they would never be viewed with the same respect that they should.

There is a unique demographic situation occurring now. There are about 20 million "silent generation" people, 77 million boomers, 10 million Gen X'ers and 76 million Millennials. There are members of the silent generation that are respectable people with a number of incredible accomplishments. However, they are often resistant to technology and lack credibility because of it. It pains me to see these people slowly losing credibility.

The same is true for some boomers. Some boomers get it. Others are trying to create an environment that makes them comfortable. Sadly, this is often at odds with the current realities of economic uncertainty, an action-oriented approach to business and the clear charge to work smarter AND harder.

My advice: If you want to be respected and relevant, you need to understand the importance of technology. Learn it. Apply it. Speak it. Your efforts will pay off as you are included in conversations that include technology and current business practices. Your skills are needed but you must communicate and function as it is now. Not like it used to be.

74.   Learn new technology tools.

75.   Master at least one.

The Adoption Curve and Digital Marketing

Digital Marketing is a broad term that refers to any type of marketing that has a primarily electronic or internet-focus for delivery or content. Included in Digital Marketing are websites, email marketing, search engine optimization, social networking, blogging, pay per click advertising, banner ads, podcasts, and other ways to reach your audience on-line. But, why should you care?

Why should you care? New technology tools are adopted in the stages as laid out by Geoffrey Moore in "Crossing the Chasm", going from innovators to early adopters to early majority to late majority and, then, finally to laggards. Early adopters get the most benefit from applying the tools correctly, learning the ins and outs of the tools, and then, capitalizing on their early adopter status. For example, many people were impressed if you had a website in the early-mid 90's. The early websites were able to capture new markets, appeal to new types of buyers, and the brand was perceived as fresh and modern. Now, if you don't have a website, you are considered archaic and, hopelessly, anachronistic.

The same is true for social networking, blogging, and other Digital Marketing tools now. The most benefit went to the early adopters. The early adopters must have patience and be willing to stub their toe on a few of the technologies that may not survive but there is a huge opportunity for the early and the brave.

The most important thing to remember about digital marketing is that the same rules of classic marketing apply, know your customer, deliver a message that will inspire them to act, and be consistent. Demand a return on your marketing investment. Any digital marketing tool can be either terrific or disastrous depending upon the results you receive that correlate directly to your business goals.

76.   Take inventory of your digital marketing.

77.   Answer the question, 'what's working?'

78.   Identify a new technology.

79.   Learn how it applies to your business.

80.   Pilot the technology.

Integrity, the Economy, and People Changing

While working for IBM between 1999 and 2002, during the dotcom boom and bust, I noticed that people change when the economy Steps. I am seeing it again in Phoenix as the real estate, development, and construction industry has gone bust.

I have had countless people call me and talk to me about:

a) Being thrown under the proverbial bus as times are getting tougher

b) Integrity and ethics becoming very loose and flexible

c) Losing their jobs without a skill set that they can apply in the new economy

Words of wisdom:

a) You are who you are regardless of the times...the tougher the economy or circumstances...the more likely you are to show your true self.

b) Integrity is not relative. Period.

c) It is up to each employee and employer to keep their skills sharp. Even when it's busy. Especially when it's not.

81. Decide how you will conduct business.

82. Ensure all aspects of your business are consistently employing your chosen approach.

Owning A Business Is Like Having Three Personalities!

After an extremely busy four months, I have re-emerged from the "office zone." As a business owner, it is nearly impossible to avoid getting pulled into the day to day duties that come with working in the business. Keeping a focus ON the business is challenging but necessary.

The first challenge of business ownership that I have recently experienced is being caught in functionally running a business. Many people who get stuck in this role have a job not a business. They are technicians and experts but generally the business does not yield an asset at the end of its useful life. At this level there is despair and, yet, independence.

The second aspect of business ownership is the process of working on the business; working on it to grow it and learn how to run it efficiently. There is terror here as one learns and grows out of the comfort zone into new areas.

The third level is visionary and leader. This aspect of entrepreneurship is exciting and very conceptual. The E-Myth refers to these three levels as Technician, Manager, and Visionary.

A successful business owner must mindfully and carefully blend all three in just the right amounts in order to successfully grow the business while maintaining personal sanity and growing an asset for future abundance.

83.   Evaluate your roles. Are you effectively functioning in all three?

Let's Be Honest...Do You Really Believe in Your Client?

What I loved about owning a marketing firm was the opportunity to support people's vision and goals for their life and their business. When the client's vision was clear, when the company had integrity, when everything clicked, the relationship was a true joy. The value was clear to everyone. However, sometimes client relationships aren't that consistent.

It's a fit!

Working with the clients whom we believe in and love to serve is truly a privilege. We find ourselves bending over backwards for these people. We cheer their successes and commiserate with their disappointments. The opportunity to be a part of someone's future and growth is not a role we take lightly. After all, a marketing company helps you get where you want to go. Your marketing partner should be your cheerleader, your support and your friend. They should be candid enough to tell you that your ideas won't support your goal and caring enough to believe in you when you are struggling to believe in yourself. Whether our client is a person in a large company or the owner of a small firm, the natural "values fit" must be there in order for exponential growth to occur.

Moving on....

When a client is rude, disrespectful and unprofessional, it is easy to agree to move on. But what if the problem isn't so obvious? What if the culture is just not aligned? What if the way the client communicates, the beliefs they hold about marketing or the way they treat marketing is just not a fit? It's tough (especially on payroll weeks) but I say the right approach is to wish them well and provide referrals to other firms where they may be better aligned. In the end, it's better for your client and better for you. It is a respectful and kind act to sacrifice revenue so that the client can be happier and better served. It is also a leap in the right direction as you set the direction of your firm. I am taking a stand by saying, "It must be done."

Believe and care. Or, let go.

84. **List your clients.**

85. **Answer the questions, "Do I like them? Do I believe in them?"**

86. **If the answer is no, let them go.**

Competition

Recently I realized that one of my competitors had "shopped" me and employed others to gain competitive information about my business. This same competitor and I used to be friends. However, about the time I started my firm, instead of a friendly and collaborative "coopetition," the relationship was completely severed. Is this inevitable in a competitive business situation?

I don't think so. I believe that the truly "great" firms, the so-called "giants" in their industries are strengthened by competition and possess a mutual respect and appreciation for the competitions' strengths and value. They understand that there is rarely just one firm in a niche. I also believe that the hallmark of a respected leader is to rise above pettiness and find a way to create a positive, win-win relationship.

As a software salesperson at IBM, I frequently navigated the competitive waters of hardware reps unhappy that the IBM database software I sold sat on a Sun server. I also understood when the RS6000 server reps created relationships with the Oracle reps. Yet, at the end of the day, we understood that ethics, integrity, and professionalism were more important than the "brand" of the day.

When I started my marketing firm, several people, including some "competitors" were gracious and helpful. Some of them even referred me work! I will always be grateful and will go out of my way to assist them anytime. In fact, I have even referred some of them work! Long-term relationships are built on mutual respect and coopetition.

87.   Identify your competitors.

88.   Take them to lunch.

Taking a Break!

Creativity is a broad term that covers all the normal things like art and architecture but everyone is creative in their own way. Whether someone writes, manages people, or promotes a business, the ability to access the creative and fresh ideas inside of oneself is extremely important.

I have always been one of those work, work, work people. I grew up with a few but not regular family vacations and even now, my mother, generally thinks vacations are a waste of time. I disagree. Going on vacation is like powering down your computer to clear the cache. When you clear the cache, the computer works better and faster after the "reboot."

Study after study shows that time is required for creative people to access their creativity. I would argue that everyone is creative and requires these breaks. And, I would further assert that the break should involve a connection with nature. We are so technologically focused that a refocus on nature and a connection with the organic rhythms is essential for us to connect with our fundamental self. And, it provides us with a new pool of creative ideas and a fresh source for new approaches. If you haven't already, make a commitment to take a break and replenish your creativity and your connection to nature.

89.   Take a break.

Marketing is a PROFESSION!

May I briefly get on my marketing soapbox? Marketing is a profession, just like law, accounting, architecture, engineering, and medicine is a profession. Why don't professional service practitioners believe that?

During my 20+ year career in marketing and sales, I have stumbled upon two key beliefs and perceptions that make me CRAZY! One, is that salespeople have to be pushy to be successful. (Not true but I'm not going to address in this post.) The other, especially in professional service firms, is a belief that marketing is an administrative function without real discipline.

Because so many professional service firms were not legally allowed to market for many years, the professionals themselves were required to bring business in the door. Those "rainmaking" professionals were compensated higher and put on partnership tracks faster than those who could not generate business. Unfortunately, as marketing has become more accepted in professional service firms, there is still a pervasive belief that marketing professional services is little more than taking someone to lunch or the golf course. Business development and marketing are confused and marketing "professionals" are looked upon as glorified administrative assistants.

Marketing professionals went to school to learn marketing (which is an all-inclusive category that includes advertising, sales, brochures, websites, strategy, planning, analysis, branding, pricing, etc.) Marketing professionals do more than take people to lunch, buy ads or design graphics. The marketing PROFESSION is one that combines the intricacies of psychology, the analysis of business, the knowledge of technology and trends, and the creativity of design. It is a complex profession that requires a variety of skills developed after years of practice and experience...not unlike other professional services.

A marketing professional knows that they are not going to handle accounting, design a building or write a brief. Why do these professionals think they can market?

First, it is because most professionals don't understand what marketing is. Many people confuse marketing with advertising, PR, or branding. Few understand the entire realm of marketing and the process and analytics that underscore a strong marketing effort.

Second, just like someone who buys a digital camera thinks they can pass on hiring a professional photographer, anyone who has viewed an advertisement on TV or taken a prospective client to lunch thinks they know marketing.

Third, marketing professionals have confused the world by not clearly defining it. They interchange the words advertising, PR, graphic design and sales all the time. It creates more confusion about the depth and complexity of the marketing profession.

So, a special plea to professional service providers. Please view your marketing professionals as just that...professionals. If they are not professionals, hire a consultant to help you understand what marketing strategy, planning, execution and analysis can provide your firm.

I'm getting off my soapbox now.

90. You don't cut your own hair. Hire marketing professionals.

The Wrecking of a Brand

Creating a brand is a special and precious endeavor. It creates a promise, an expectation, and a level of commitment that is unique and wonderful. Ellen Tracy clothing was one of those types of brands.

I wore Ellen Tracy clothing for many years. Ellen Tracy clothing was the combination of quality, style, and professionalism. I LOVED the brand. Although I couldn't afford it at retail prices, I flocked to the sale racks and wore the brand proudly.

During the "Great Recession," I saw a disheartening situation. Whoever purchased the Ellen Tracy brand has decided to wreck it. The labels, the design, and the material choices are all terrible. Where Ellen Tracy used to be the hallmark of stylish professionalism, it is now frumpy old lady clothing carried only by a few large department stores. What happened? It is so sad, so unnecessary...such a probable choice of economics over branding. It's a sad, sad situation. A brand should be cherished; cared for, treasured...the promise of the brand is something not to be taken lightly. Yet, in this case, it seems economics has trumped brand consistency. Who is buying this new brand promise? I can't imagine someone wrecking a brand more thoroughly....What a shame!

Remember; be true to your brand. Hold its promise carefully in your hands. It is a responsibility to be treasured.

91. **Answer this question: What is your brand promise?**

Sometimes We Get Too Comfortable...

If you have valued clients, slowly but surely you can begin to slip up or take them for granted or notice the things that bother you to the point where you begin building a case in your head for parting company. Don't do it! Read this first!

Just like a personal relationship, sometimes we can get just a little too cozy, sloppy or lazy to stay as sharp and crisp as we were at the beginning of the relationship. Maybe deadlines start to slip. Maybe materials aren't as crisp. Maybe we don't tell our clients how much we appreciate them.

It's human to get tired, worn out or occasionally complacent. Then, we start to justify the reason the relationship isn't working by getting irritated with the client's habits or shortfalls.

1. Try this as a marketing strategy or client retention tool, write a list or consciously notice what you appreciate about your clients and then, tell them! By offering appreciation not only will it reaffirm your commitment to them but it will likely create more goodwill. Eighty percent of your business will come from twenty percent of your clients. Keep those twenty percent happy and growing!

2. Be honest with yourself about your shortfalls. And, then, improve your work.

3. Know that clients and people come in and out of your business for a reason. Be okay with that flow.

Don't be too hard on yourself but stay sharp! Competitors who are hungry are doing everything they can to capitalize on service failures.

92.   Identify your top 20% of customers.

93.   List the things you appreciate about them.

94.   List your shortcomings.

95.   Improve.

96.   Get comfortable with the dynamic nature of customers coming and going.

Small Fish in a Shrinking Pond or Growing Fish Seeking Deeper Waters?

There is a phenomenon I am beginning to recognize as I meet an increasing number of clients and we mutually evaluate whether or not there is a good "fit" between us. The phenomenon is this: some clients are small fish that want to feel like big fish so they unconsciously but deliberately *SHRINK* their ponds. They are not really open to new ideas, experts, or plans for growth because they desperately want to maintain or shrink their pond. Sometimes that pond becomes polluted or uncomfortably small and then they are forced to seek new waters. Often, they are just looking for another small pond so they can be a big fish again. Small fish in shrinking ponds will always work against a growing fish seeking deeper waters.

Growing fish on the other hand are curious, eager, and optimistic. They know that the next bigger, deeper body of water will provide better food, more fun, and yet another opportunity to go to an even bigger body of water. When evaluating clients, the decision is this, are they a small fish that is shrinking their world in order to feel like a large fish or are they a growing fish seeking deeper waters?

The challenge is that often the small fish are masquerading as growing fish. When they decide to hire marketing firms (or hire new proactive staff) they start off as presenting themselves as growing fish. They say they want to grow their pond or find deeper waters but they are fundamentally petrified of deeper waters. They cannot "be" with the knowledge that they are not the biggest fish in the pond. They spend all the time with the marketing company (or person with their organization) working to recreate the small pond in which they were the big fish. They reject growth strategies, they avoid new markets, and they spend a great deal of time telling everyone or showing everyone that they are big fish. These people usually end up letting go of their marketing consultants or new proactive staff because they cannot handle the fundamental objective of growing their pond.

It is a phenomenon we sometimes see in our families. Someone wants to be the expert, the most knowledgeable or the most accomplished but they are confronted by another family member who is a growing fish diving into deeper waters. How do they maintain the "illusion" that they are a big fish? They can't and it's darn uncomfortable. They have spent the year(s) shrinking their pond so that they feel like a big fish every day. Their staff, their home life, their friends have been carefully chosen to maintain the illusion that they are big fish. Then, during the holidays, they must contend with someone who has continued to grow by seeking deeper and bigger waters to strengthen themselves. They don't know how to "be" with a growing fish except try to attack or limit the growth of the growing fish or try to eliminate it from their pond. They do this by questioning or attacking the growing fish's compelling urge to grow. They don't want to shrink the growing fish's pond, because then, they will have to compete with the growing fish for the same waters. Instead, they try to make the growing fish feel uncertain, small or vulnerable.

The challenge for the growing fish is that it often doesn't feel like it is ever a "big fish." It must be comfortable with the uncertain nature of growth. It knows it's growing but by its very nature, it will continue to seek bigger waters until it is a whale in the ocean. Does a whale in the ocean feel large? Compared to the vastness around it, probably not. Yet, compared to the tiniest of ocean fish, it recognizes its enormity.

Are you a big fish seeking deeper waters or a small fish trying to shrink your pond?

97. Decide the type of fish you want to be.

How Important Is It To Be Nice?

Many people were raised with the notion that it's important to be a "nice girl" or a "nice boy." Then, came the books, "Nice guys finish last" or "Good girls don't get the corner office."

So, let me understand this...if you are nice, you are an unpromotable wimp...but if you are nasty you will be a successful jerk? Come again?

Surely, there is some middle ground here. As a parent of a teenager and a business owner, I understand that I can't be a pushover but I also tend to lead with pleasantness, interest, and understanding when I am meeting with people. People are interesting, generally good, and have their own doubts about their competence and expertise.

It's a winning strategy to start with respect and lead with friendship. If you find the treatment is not mutual, reevaluate your approach. I say it's time to have books that are titled, "Be nice. Be good. And, be successful!"

98. Be nice.

I Love Lady Gaga, Katy Perry, and Taylor Swift...

And my daughter thinks it's lame. "Mom, you're old. You CAN'T like Lady Gaga," she declared.

I DO like Lady Gaga and it's partially because of the parallels to my beliefs about marketing.

Marketing should be authentic, fresh, appeal to its audience, exploit technology, be exciting, and have energy. Lady Gaga is all that.

She is authentic and talented. She has taken risks that have paid off. She has also worked hard from her beginnings as a 4-year old piano protégé. Marketing approaches should be similar. They should be authentic, take measured risks, and build from history and quality.

Lady Gaga is fresh, exciting, and energetic. Marketing should be the same. Even "tired" brands pitched to "seasoned" audiences can be charged with new life when marketed with a sense of excitement, verve, and loft.

Can you say, "Technology pays"? Lady Gaga is controlling and growing her brand via technology. Her latest video is right there and available for purchase. There is no escaping the opportunity to buy her product. Her website is extraordinarily rich with content and yet, lean. Everything on the site adds to the experience of the fan. And, there is nothing extra that detracts from the experience of, well, experiencing Lady Gaga.

So, my daughter may think it's inappropriate for her forty-something mom to like Lady Gaga but I do. She is talented, exciting, and artistic. I applaud her as I encourage marketers to follow her example of authenticity, talent, smarts, and artistry.

99. Be an original!

Lessons Learned as a Business Owner

My years as a business owner shaped me. They taught me more than my Master of Business Administration. Each challenge, opportunity, and interaction taught me important lessons that not applied to my life but to my future business conduct.

- A good business model that is executed with integrity and passion can thrive in any economy.
- Integrity, values, structure, and a constant attention to learning are the most important aspects of running a successful business.
- Choose what you want to do and then sell, sell, sell. Things have a way of working out.
- Through thick or thin...it is critical to keep your integrity and values intact.
- A strong team is absolutely critical to support the vision of a thriving, profitable business.
- Generosity and service does not always breed respect, loyalty or reciprocity. In fact, sometimes it breeds the opposite.
- Boundaries are critical to running a successful business.

- Every business has its own unique and special culture. Some clients will fit and some won't. That's as it should be.
- The best clients are the ones that respect you, are aligned with your values, and are willing to collaborate with you.
- Tend to your business as though it were a child. Then, let it go, as though it is grown.

99 Steps

1. Describe your 'brand.'

2. Create a profile of your ideal customer

3. Identify your value proposition (what makes your business special or different from the competition)

4. Develop messaging that persuasively describes your value proposition to your ideal customer

5. Incorporate the messaging into your brand.

6. Use a One-page business plan

7. Decide your core values

8. Set out your Big, Hairy, Audacious Goals

9. Describe the measures or metrics you will use to measure your success.

10. Write a mission statement.

11. Develop three goals that include specifics like revenue, costs, and timelines.

12. Answer the question 'how will you achieve these goals?'

13. Identify your niche.

14. Articulate your strategy.

15. List the tactics you will use to support your marketing strategy.

16. Create a marketing plan

17. Create a sales plan

18. Learn a new marketing tactic.

19. Call two more potential customers.

20. Call your existing customers and thank them for their business.

21. Write and submit a proposal to a new client.

22. Write and submit a press release that pegs a newsworthy item to your company's activities.

23. Host a lunch, happy hour, or party at your offices.

24. Identify two juicy words to describe your firm's value.

25. Create a style guide for your logo and brand.

26. Know your ideal client demographic.

27. Write one authentic statement about your business.

28. Create buyer profiles

29. Discover how your buyers communicate and buy.

30. Decide who you are

31. Set marketing goals.

32. Create a communication plan

33. Create a list of the marketing tactics you are currently using.

34. Ask yourself, do they reach my ideal customer?

35. Get a DUNS#

36. Register with CCR

37. Register with FedBizOpps

38. Register with ORCA

39. Prepare a qualification statement

40. Submit a request for proposal.

41. Request a debrief after the contract is awarded.

42. Explore new and different print strategies.

43. Identify awards that you can pursue.

44. Submit applications to at least one of them.

45. Create a blog

46. Weave key words into the content

47. List your company with Google Local Business, Yahoo Local Business, and the Yellow Pages.

48. Explore Search Engine Optimization

49. Install Google Analytics on your website.

50. Conduct a review of your digital marketing strategies. Answer the questions: Are they meeting your objectives? Do they generate leads?

51. Register your site on these website ranking websites.

52. Open a personal LinkedIn account.

53. Create a company page on FaceBook.

54. Install a content management system or if you already have one, ensure at least one person uses it weekly to update the site.

55. Proactively decide your approach to social media. How often do you want to post? What will the content be?

56. Get to know Google.

57. Refresh your website.

58. Create an avatar.

59. Review your web analytics.

60. Identify five key words for your business.

61. Register with at least two internet directories.

62. Measure your website analytics.

63. Try a new social media site.

64. Use email marketing.

65. Try a list swap with another firm.

66. Identify key words people use to search for your business.

67. Read a blog.

68. Choose one additional niche for your company to pursue.

69. Pick up the phone or write a note to someone with whom you have always wanted to work. Be authentic. Ask for their business.

70. Determine if you are B2B or B2C.

71. Does your marketing approach support your niche? Or, are you attempting to use B2C marketing approaches for a B2B firm?

72. Identify ONE thing to improve your marketing.

73. Do it.

74. Learn new technology tools.

75. Master at least one.

76. Take inventory of your digital marketing.

77. Answer the question, 'what's working?'

78. Identify a new technology.

79. Learn how it applies to your business.

80. Pilot the technology.

81. Decide how you will conduct business.

82. Ensure all aspects of your business are consistently employing your chosen approach.

83. Evaluate your roles. Are you effectively functioning in all three?

84. List your clients.

85. Answer the questions, "Do I like them? Do I believe in them?"

86. If the answer is no, let them go.

87. Identify your competitors.

88. Take them to lunch.

89. Take a break.

90. You don't cut your own hair. Hire marketing professionals.

91. Answer this question: What is your brand promise?

92. Identify your top 20% of customers.

93. List the things you appreciate about them.

94. List your shortcomings.

95. Improve.

96. Get comfortable with the dynamic nature of customers coming and going.

97. Decide the type of fish you want to be.

98. Be nice.

99. Be an original.

Thank you for reading Smart Marketing. I sincerely hope it was beneficial to you. Please leave a review on Amazon or GoodReads. I would love to know your opinion.

Also, please visit my website, www.andreakamenca.com. If you leave your email address, you will be able to access special gifts including some of the quotes and forms. If you want to share how the book impacted you, I would be delighted to hear about it!

Andrea

www.ingramcontent.com/pod-product-compliance
Lightning Source LLC
Chambersburg PA
CBHW060047210326
41520CB00009B/1298